Look at the picture. What do you see?

Who do you think broke the cookie jar?

Was it the dog? Was it the cat?
Was it Grandma or Joe? Look at the
paw prints among the pieces of the
cookie jar? Are the paw prints big or
little?

Do you think that the cat broke the jar? If so, you are right. Good for you!
    That's what a detective does. A detective works at figuring out what happened.

The paw prints by the broken cookie jar were a clue. A clue helps you tell what happened.

Detectives always look for clues.

Sometimes, you can't find a clue by just looking. There may be none around. Instead, you can ask people questions. This might lead you to the right answer.

There are different kinds of detectives. Some are police officers. They help solve crimes.

Another type of detective is a private detective. People pay private detectives to find lost people and things.

Would you like to be a detective?